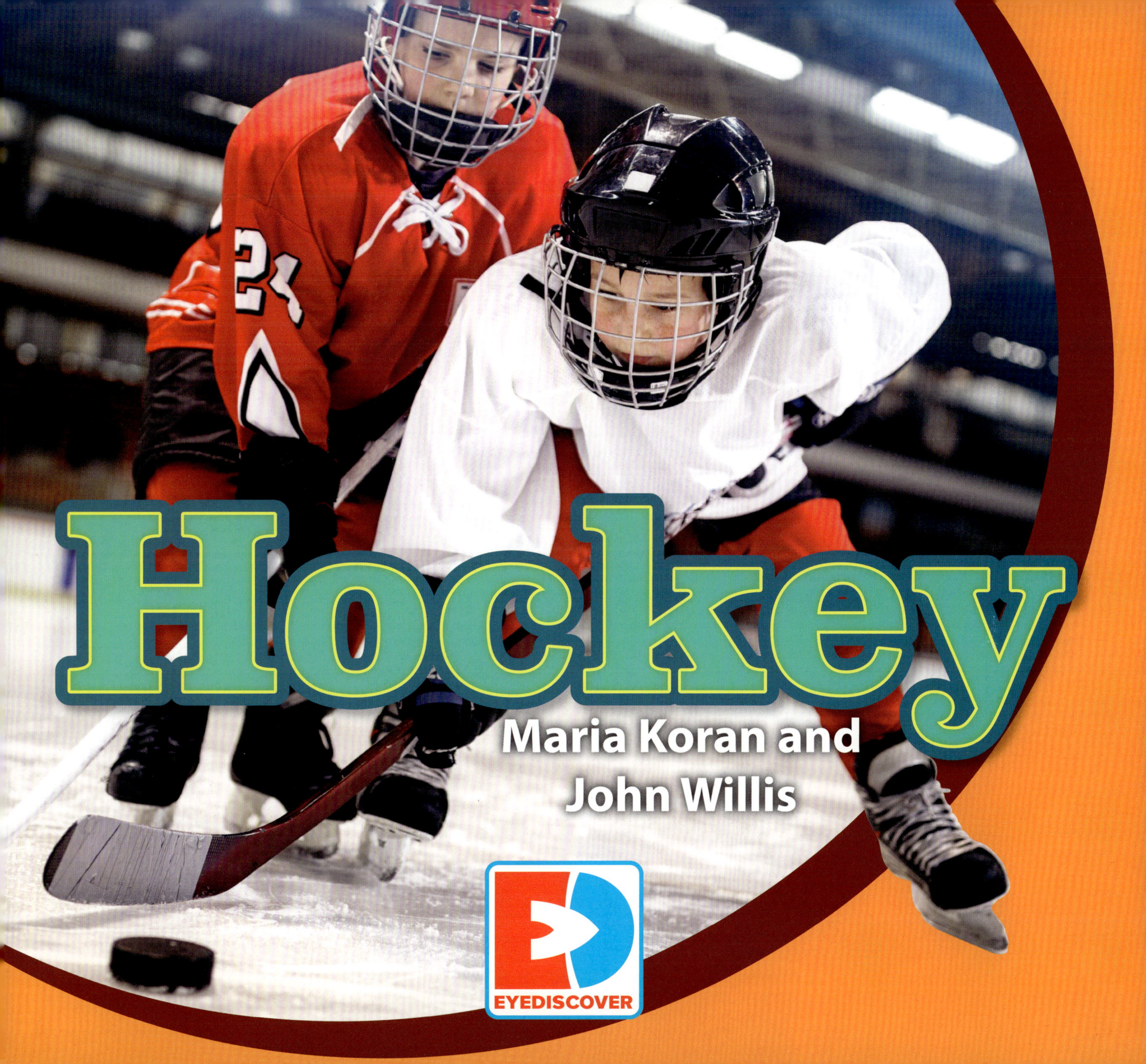

Hockey

Maria Koran and
John Willis

EYEDISCOVER

Go to www.eyediscover.com and enter this book's unique code.

BOOK CODE

AVF96827

EYEDISCOVER brings you optic readalongs that support active learning.

Published by AV2
276 5th Avenue, Suite 704 #917
New York, NY 10001
Website: www.eyediscover.com

Library of Congress Control Number: 2021937103

ISBN 978-1-7911-3990-2 (hardcover)

Printed in Guangzhou, China
1 2 3 4 5 6 7 8 9 0 25 24 23 22 21

042021
102120

Project Coordinator: John Willis
Designer: Mandy Christiansen

The publisher acknowledges Getty Images, Alamy, and Dreamstime as the primary image suppliers for this title.

EYEDISCOVER provides enriched content, optimized for tablet use, that supplements and complements this book. EYEDISCOVER books strive to create inspired learning and engage young minds in a total learning experience.

Watch
Video content brings each page to life.

Browse
Thumbnails make navigation simple.

Read
Follow along with text on the screen.

Listen
Hear each page read aloud.

Your EYEDISCOVER Optic Readalongs come alive with...

Audio
Listen to the entire book read aloud.

Video
High resolution videos turn each spread into an optic readalong.

OPTIMIZED FOR

- TABLETS
- WHITEBOARDS
- COMPUTERS
- AND MUCH MORE!

This title is part of our EyeDiscover digital subscription

1-Year EyeDiscover Subscription
ISBN 978-1-4896-8346-5

Access all EyeDiscover titles with our digital subscription. Sign up for a FREE trial at www.eyediscover.com/trial

Hockey

In this book, you will learn about

- what it is
- how it is played
- where it is played

and much more!

Hockey is a team sport. It is played on ice. Hockey players wear skates to move around.

Hockey is played using a puck. A hockey puck is made of rubber.

Hockey players use hockey sticks to move the puck and shoot it.

Players shoot the puck into the other team's net to score. The team with the highest score when the game ends wins.

Goaltenders wear heavy gear. They try to keep the puck out of their team's net.

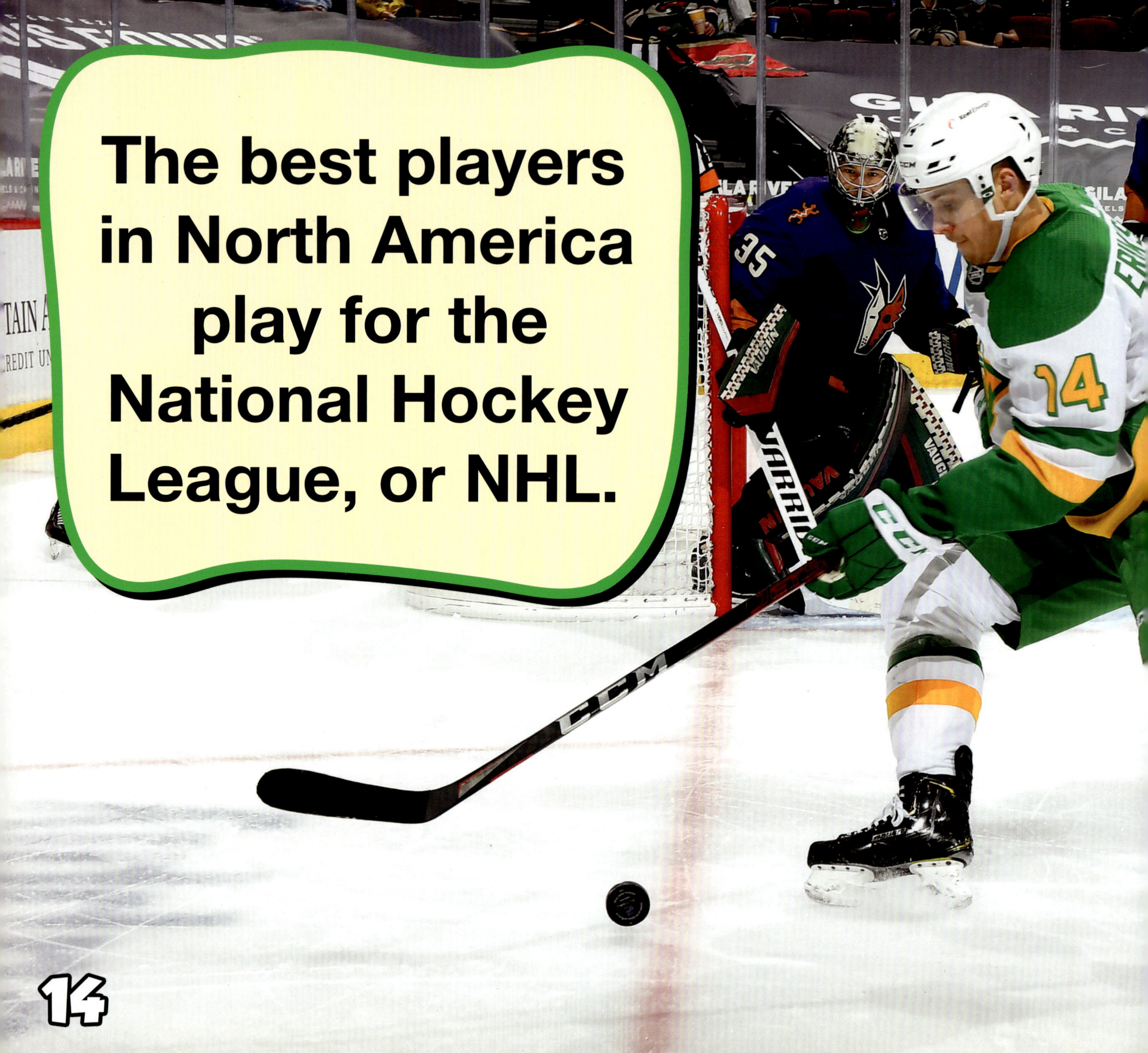

The best players in North America play for the National Hockey League, or NHL.

GILA RIVER
HOTELS & CASINOS
CCM

NHL players play for the Stanley Cup. This trophy is named after a man called Lord Stanley of Preston.

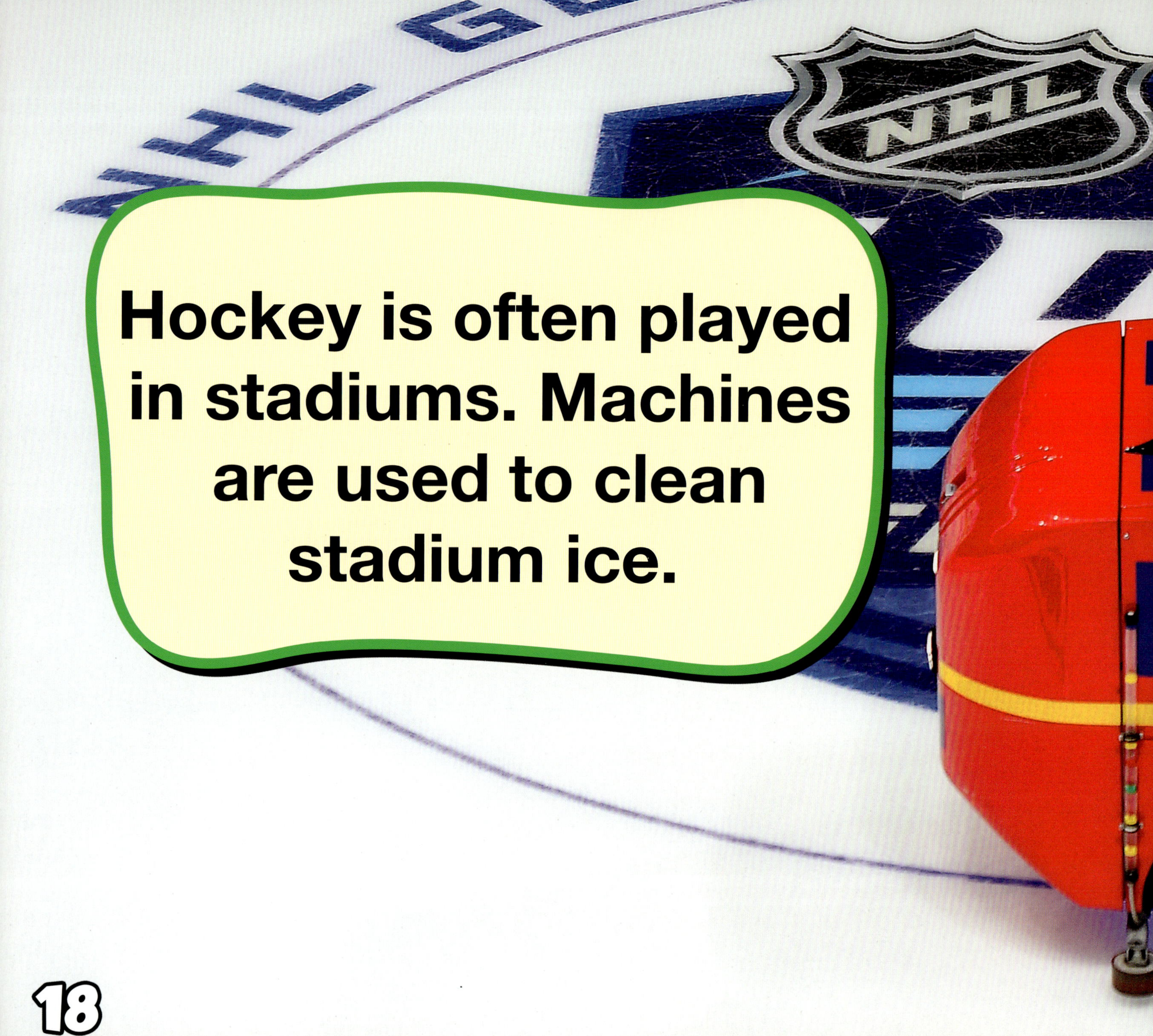

Hockey is often played in stadiums. Machines are used to clean stadium ice.

GLOBAL SERIES FINLAND · 2018
GLOBAL SERIES FINLAND · 2018
Helmi
GLOBAL SERIES FINLAND · 2018
OLYMPIA
8
ICEBEAR
Electric

HEAD

Hockey can be played outside, too. Many people enjoy hockey games on frozen lakes.

HOCKEY BY THE NUMBERS

A **hockey team** usually has **six players** on the ice **at a time.**

A **GOALTENDER** may wear about **40 pounds** (18 kilograms) of **equipment.**

Modern **hockey pucks** were **first used** around **1875**.

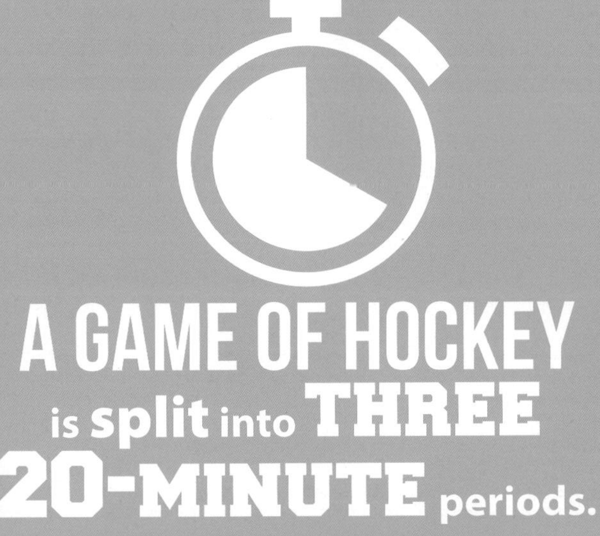

A GAME OF HOCKEY is **split** into **THREE 20-MINUTE** periods.

An **NHL hockey rink** is **200 feet** (61 meters) **long** and **85 feet** (26 m) **wide**.

The **NHL** was formed more than **100 years ago**.

KEY WORDS

Research has shown that as much as 65 percent of all written material published in English is made up of 300 words. These 300 words cannot be taught using pictures or learned by sounding them out. They must be recognized by sight. This book contains 37 common sight words to help young readers improve their reading fluency and comprehension. This book also teaches young readers several important content words, such as proper nouns. These words are paired with pictures to aid in learning and improve understanding.

Page	Sight Words First Appearance
4	a, around, is, it, move, on, to
7	made, of
8	and, the, use
10	ends, into, other, when, with
13	keep, out, their, they, try
14	America, for, in, or, play
17	after, man, this
18	are, often
21	be, can, many, people, too

Page	Content Words First Appearance
4	hockey, ice, players, skates, sport
7	puck, rubber
8	hockey sticks
10	game, net, score
13	gear, goaltenders
14	National Hockey League, North America
17	Lord Stanley of Preston, Stanley Cup, trophy
18	machines, stadiums
21	lakes, outside

Watch
Video content brings each page to life.

Browse
Thumbnails make navigation simple.

Read
Follow along with text on the screen.

Listen
Hear each page read aloud.

Go to www.eyediscover.com and enter this book's unique code.

BOOK CODE

AVF96827